Why things don't work
MOTORBIKE

www.raintreepublishers.co.uk
Visit our website to find out more information about
Raintree books.

To order:
☎ Phone 44 (0) 1865 888113
▤ Send a fax to 44 (0) 1865 314091
▣ Visit the Raintree bookshop at
www.raintreepublishers.co.uk to browse our
catalogue and order online.

Why things don't work MOTORBIKE
was produced by

David West ⚭ Children's Books
7 Princeton Court
55 Felsham Road
London SW15 1AZ

Editor: Dominique Crowley
Consultant: Rob Harris

First published in Great Britain by
Raintree, Halley Court, Jordan Hill, Oxford OX2 8EJ, part of
Harcourt Education. Raintree is a registered trademark of Harcourt
Education Ltd.

10 digit ISBN: 1 4062 0546 X
13 digit ISBN: 978 1 4062 0546 6

11 10 09 08 07
10 9 8 7 6 5 4 3 2 1

British Library Cataloguing in Publication Data

West, David
    Motorcycle. - (Why things don't work)
    1.Motorcycles - Maintenance and repair - Comic books,
    strips, etc. - Juvenile literature
    I.Title
    629.2'8775

Printed and bound in China

Why things don't work
MOTORBIKE

by David West

Contents

6 GRANDAD'S MOTORBIKE

8 THE TWO-STROKE ENGINE

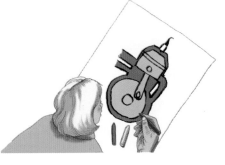

10 THE CARBURETTOR AND BATTERY

12 SPARK PLUGS AND FUEL

14 GEARBOX AND CLUTCH

16 DRIVE CHAIN AND SPROCKETS

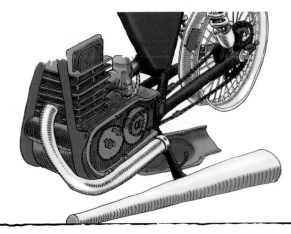

18 WHEELS AND BEARINGS

20 TYRES

22 BRAKES

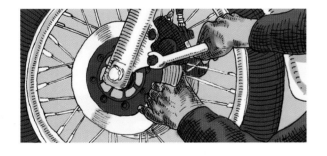

24 SUSPENSION

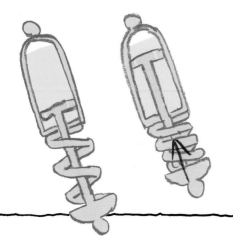

26 RIDING A MOTORBIKE

28 OTHER TYPES OF MOTORBIKE

30 PARTS OF A MOTORBIKE

31 GLOSSARY

32 INDEX

Grandad's motorbike

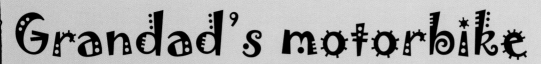

TOM AND SISSY HAVE FOUND A MOTORBIKE IN THE BARN. IT BELONGED TO TOM'S GRANDAD AND IT LOOKS AS IF IT DOES NOT WORK.

BUT WHY DOES IT NOT WORK?
COULD IT BE THAT...

THERE'S NO **FUEL** IN THE TANK.

THE SPARK PLUGS ARE DIRTY.

THE **CABLES** ARE NOT ATTACHED.

THERE IS NO OIL IN THE SUSPENSION.

THE BRAKES DO NOT WORK.

THE FRONT TYRE IS FLAT.

THE CARBURETTOR HAS FALLEN OFF.

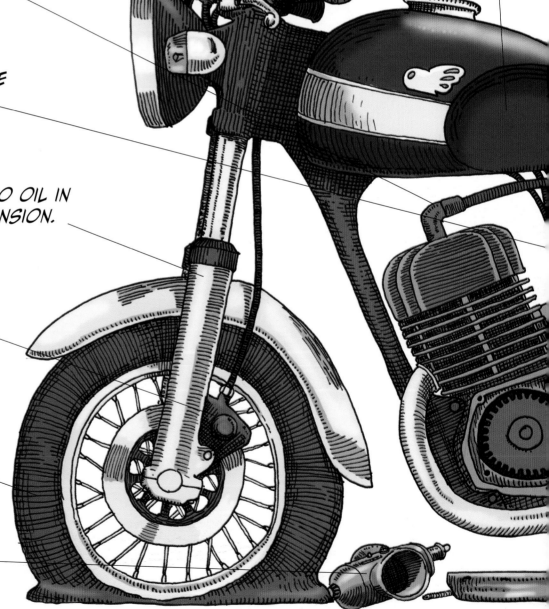

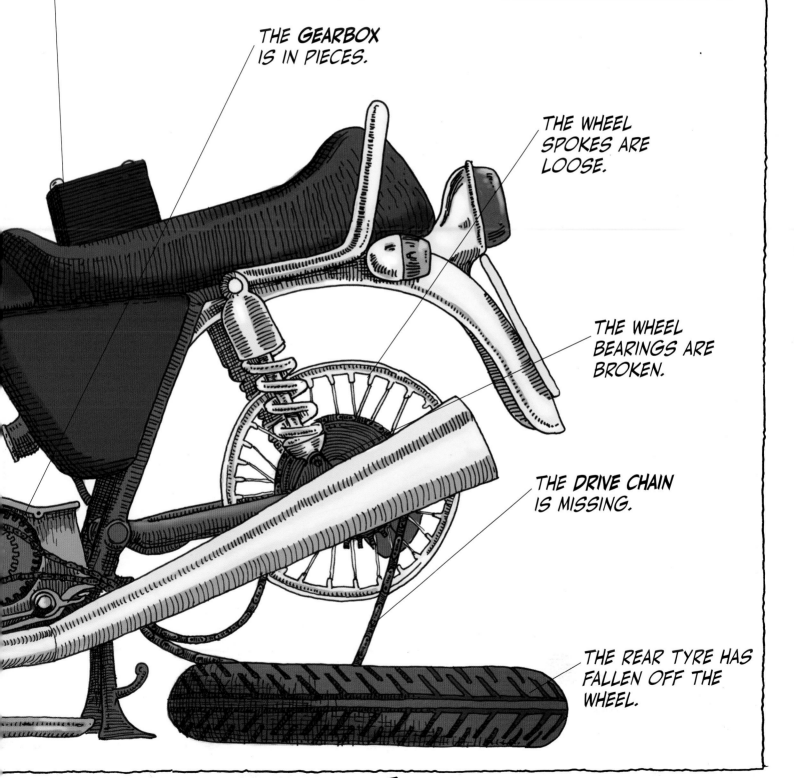

THESE ARE JUST SOME OF THE REASONS WHY THE MOTORBIKE WILL NOT WORK.

DISCOVER THE SCIENCE THAT MAKES THINGS WORK AS TOM AND SISSY SET ABOUT RESTORING GRANDAD'S MOTORBIKE.

THE **BATTERY** IS FLAT.

THE **GEARBOX** IS IN PIECES.

THE WHEEL SPOKES ARE LOOSE.

THE WHEEL BEARINGS ARE BROKEN.

THE **DRIVE CHAIN** IS MISSING.

THE REAR TYRE HAS FALLEN OFF THE WHEEL.

8

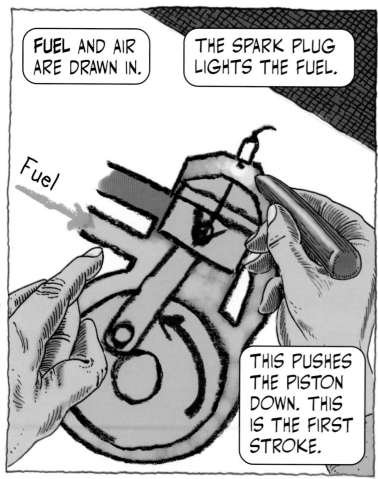

FUEL AND AIR ARE DRAWN IN.

THE SPARK PLUG LIGHTS THE FUEL.

Fuel

THIS PUSHES THE PISTON DOWN. THIS IS THE FIRST STROKE.

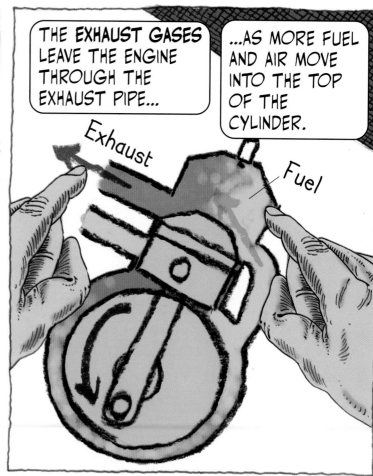

THE **EXHAUST GASES** LEAVE THE ENGINE THROUGH THE EXHAUST PIPE...

...AS MORE FUEL AND AIR MOVE INTO THE TOP OF THE CYLINDER.

Exhaust

Fuel

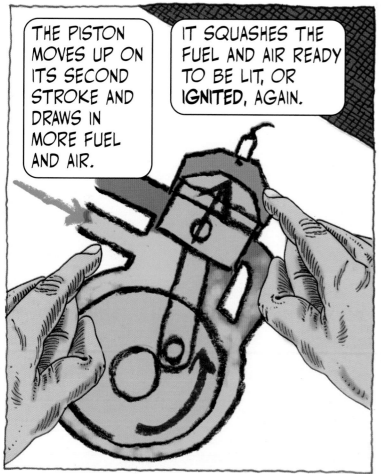

THE PISTON MOVES UP ON ITS SECOND STROKE AND DRAWS IN MORE FUEL AND AIR.

IT SQUASHES THE FUEL AND AIR READY TO BE LIT, OR **IGNITED**, AGAIN.

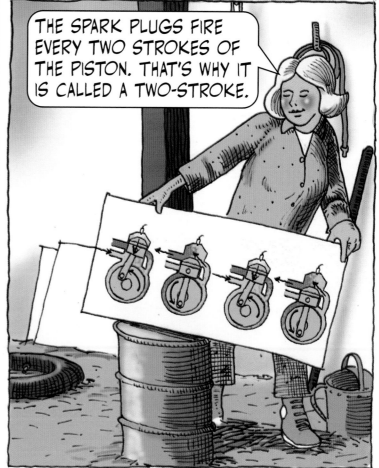

THE SPARK PLUGS FIRE EVERY TWO STROKES OF THE PISTON. THAT'S WHY IT IS CALLED A TWO-STROKE.

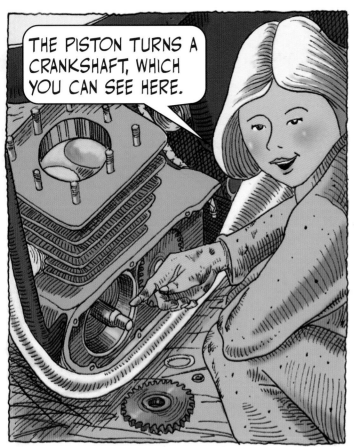

THE PISTON TURNS A CRANKSHAFT, WHICH YOU CAN SEE HERE.

WE STRIPPED DOWN THE ENGINE AND PUT IT BACK TOGETHER AGAIN.

WAIT A MINUTE. WHERE'S THE CARBURETTOR?

HERE IT IS. WITHOUT THIS THE ENGINE WON'T WORK.

YOU SEE, FUEL WON'T BURN WITHOUT AIR. THIS LITTLE DEVICE MIXES THE PETROL FUEL WITH AIR...

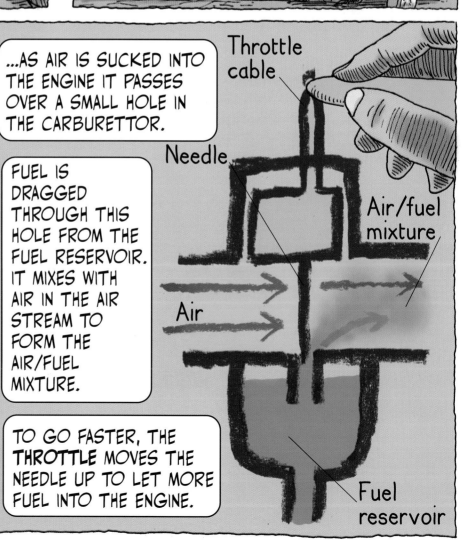

...AS AIR IS SUCKED INTO THE ENGINE IT PASSES OVER A SMALL HOLE IN THE CARBURETTOR.

FUEL IS DRAGGED THROUGH THIS HOLE FROM THE FUEL RESERVOIR. IT MIXES WITH AIR IN THE AIR STREAM TO FORM THE AIR/FUEL MIXTURE.

TO GO FASTER, THE **THROTTLE** MOVES THE NEEDLE UP TO LET MORE FUEL INTO THE ENGINE.

Throttle cable

Needle

Air/fuel mixture

Air

Fuel reservoir

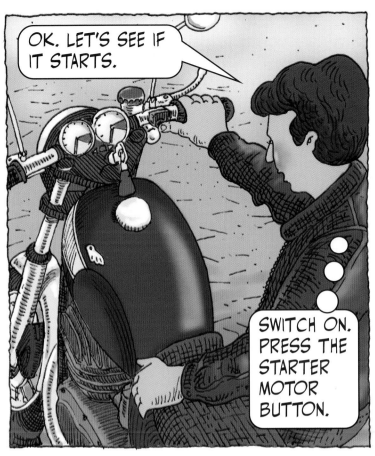

11

BUT THE ENGINE STILL WON'T START.

PERHAPS THE SPARK PLUGS AREN'T WORKING?

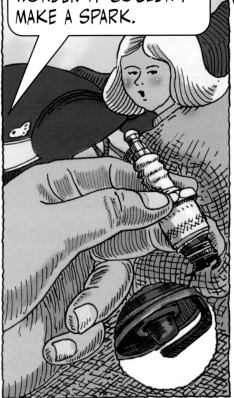

YOU'RE RIGHT. LOOK AT THAT. IT'S ALL COVERED IN SOOT FROM THE ENGINE. NO WONDER IT COULDN'T MAKE A SPARK.

WE CAN REPLACE IT WITH THIS NEW ONE. THE CLEAN METAL WILL ALLOW THE **ELECTRICITY** TO FLOW FREELY AND MAKE A BETTER SPARK.

WE HAVE TO MAKE SURE THE GAP AT THE END OF THE SPARK PLUG IS JUST RIGHT.

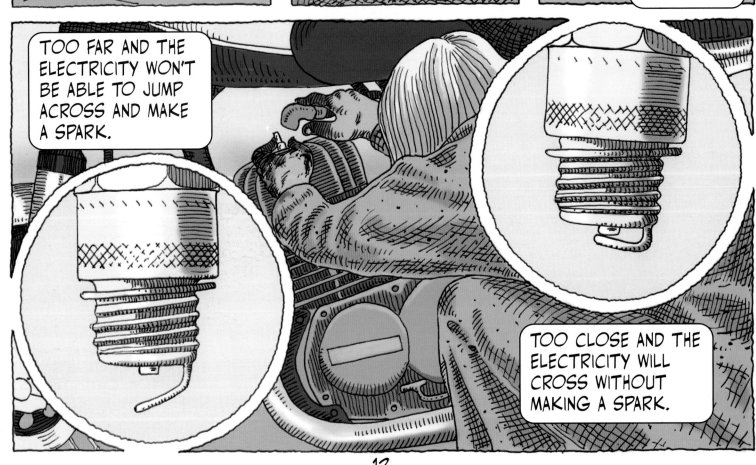

TOO FAR AND THE ELECTRICITY WON'T BE ABLE TO JUMP ACROSS AND MAKE A SPARK.

TOO CLOSE AND THE ELECTRICITY WILL CROSS WITHOUT MAKING A SPARK.

12

OK. LET'S TRY AGAIN.

JITTERJITTERTUPPER

JITTERJITTER

TOCA

FUT

I DON'T UNDERSTAND IT. WAIT A MINUTE... IS THERE PETROL IN THE TANK?

OOPS.

THERE WAS NO PETROL IN THE TANK. WE FILLED IT UP WITH PETROL AND OIL.

THE OIL HELPS LUBRICATE THE MOVING PARTS IN TWO-STROKE ENGINES.

PETROL

THIS TIME THE ENGINE FIRED UP AND TICKED OVER NICELY.

YES, THAT'S THE OIL IN THE FUEL BURNING.

PHEW! IT'S VERY SMELLY.

JITTERJITTER

TOCA

BRAAAR

14

PUTTA PUTTA

LET'S START IT UP AND TRY OUT THE GEARS.

I'LL PUSH THE LEVER DOWN FOR FIRST GEAR.

CLUNK

TUP!

THE ENGINE HAS STALLED.

DID YOU USE THE CLUTCH LEVER?

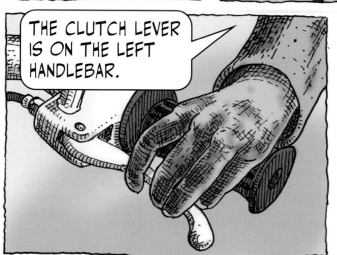

THE CLUTCH LEVER IS ON THE LEFT HANDLEBAR.

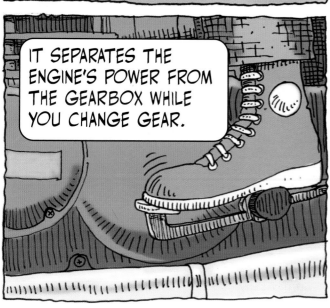

IT SEPARATES THE ENGINE'S POWER FROM THE GEARBOX WHILE YOU CHANGE GEAR.

PUTTA PUTTA

AH, THAT'S BETTER.

THE GEARS SEEM TO WORK WELL.

WHIRRR

CLUNK

PUTTA PUTTA

THE ENGINE AND GEARBOX WERE NOW WORKING.

OK. THAT'S GREAT. NOW WE NEED TO GET THE POWER TO THE BACK WHEEL.

THERE SHOULD BE A **DRIVE CHAIN** AROUND HERE SOMEWHERE.

FOUND IT.

I'VE GIVEN IT A CLEAN AND PUT SOME GREASE ON IT TO MAKE IT RUN SMOOTHLY.

FEED IT AROUND THE SPROCKET ON THE REAR WHEEL.

SPROCKET?

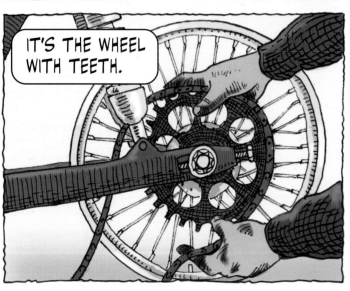

IT'S THE WHEEL WITH TEETH.

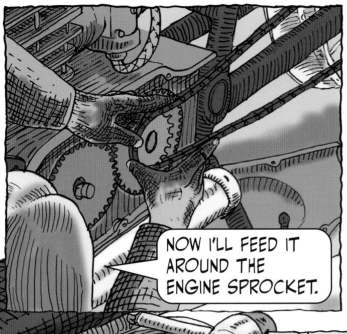

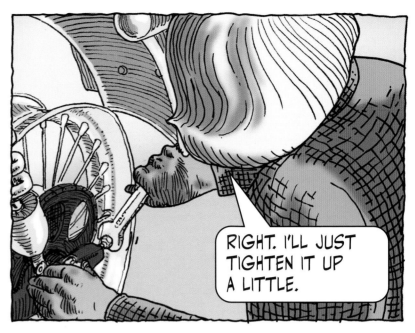

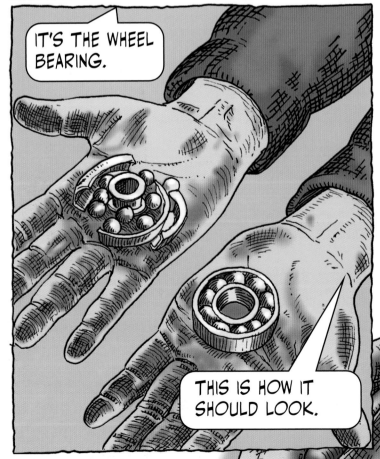

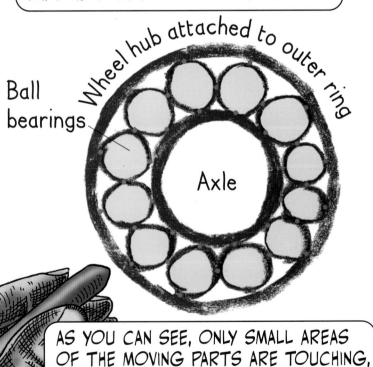

I'LL PUT IN THE NEW ONES HERE, LIKE SO...

...AND WE'LL TIGHTEN UP SOME OF THE SPOKES, WHICH HAVE COME LOOSE.

WHY DO THE WHEELS HAVE SPOKES?

IT MAKES THE WHEELS LIGHTER THAN A SOLID WHEEL. AND THAT'S IMPORTANT WHEN YOU COME TO RIDE THE BIKE.

WE PUT THE REAR WHEEL BACK ON, REATTACHED THE CHAIN, AND FIXED THE SILENCER TO THE EXHAUST PIPE.

OK. WHAT NEXT?

A NICE CUP OF TEA, I THINK.

19

Tread

21

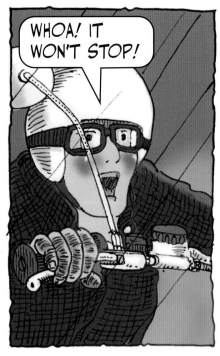

WHOA! IT WON'T STOP!

YIKES!

CRASH

ARE YOU OK?

WHAT HAPPENED?

WE TOOK THE BIKE BACK TO THE BARN, AND LOOKED AT THE BRAKES. THERE ARE THREE BRAKES: TWO DISC BRAKES ON THE FRONT AND ONE BRAKE ON THE REAR WHEEL.

IT LOOKS LIKE THE BRAKES FAILED.

WHEN YOU PRESS THE BRAKE LEVER, HYDRAULIC FLUID TRAVELS THROUGH THE BRAKE PIPES TO PUSH THE CALIPER PISTONS. THIS FORCES THE BRAKE PADS AGAINST THE BRAKE DISC TO CAUSE FRICTION. FRICTION SLOWS DOWN THE WHEELS.

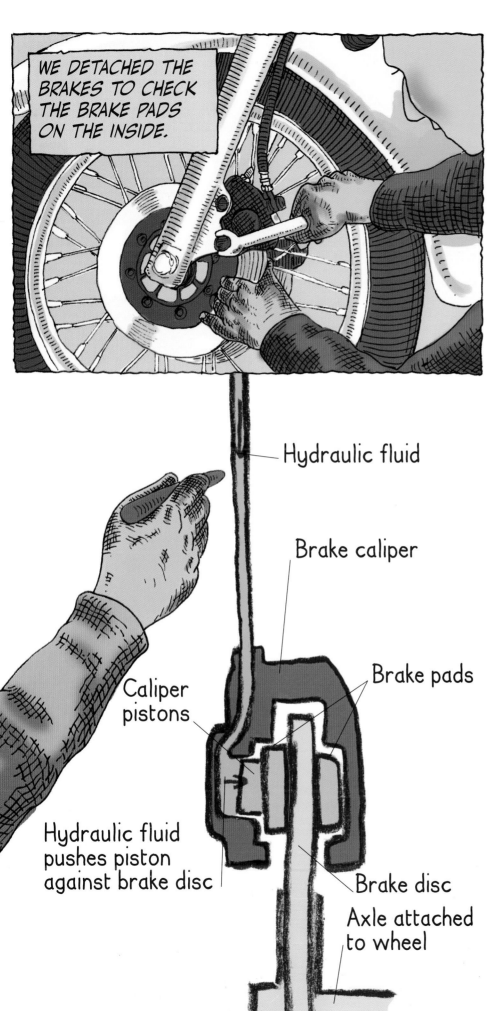

WE DETACHED THE BRAKES TO CHECK THE BRAKE PADS ON THE INSIDE.

Hydraulic fluid

Brake caliper

Caliper pistons

Brake pads

Hydraulic fluid pushes piston against brake disc

Brake disc

Axle attached to wheel

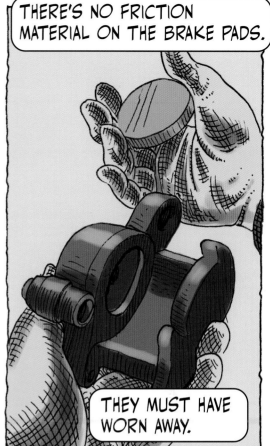

THERE'S NO FRICTION MATERIAL ON THE BRAKE PADS.

THEY MUST HAVE WORN AWAY.

WE BOUGHT SOME NEW BRAKE PADS AND FITTED THEM.

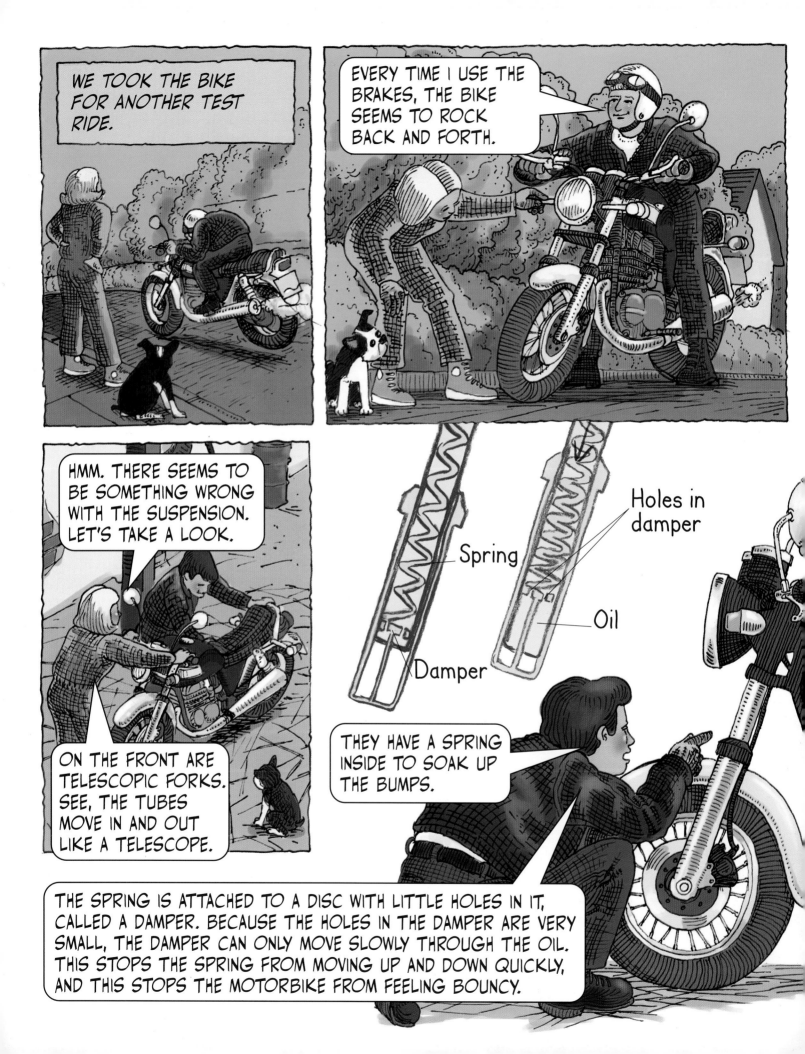

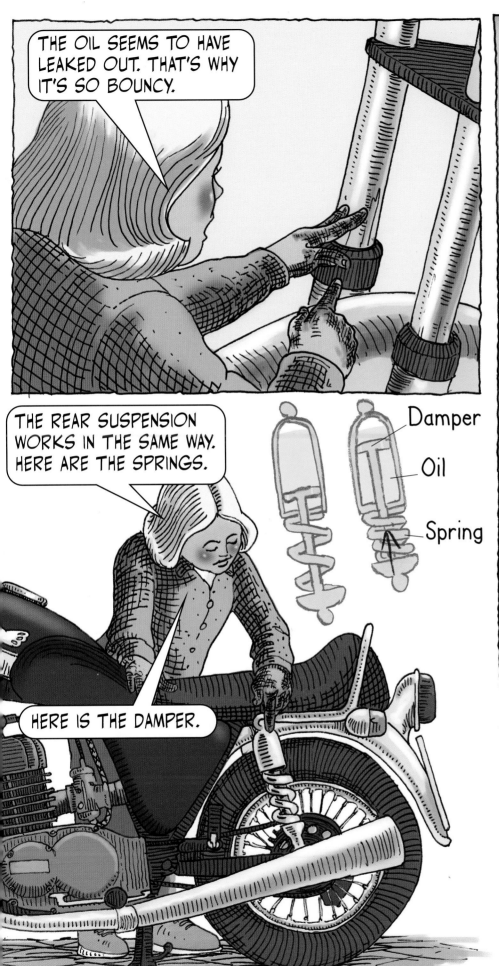

25

AFTER A WHILE...

HEY, THIS IS FUN. I'M GOING TO GO FASTER.

SLOW DOWN FOR THE CORNER!

WHOA!

CRASH

ARE YOU OK?

YES. IT WAS A SOFT LANDING.

WHEN YOU TURN A CORNER, YOU SHOULD LEAN IN TOWARDS IT.

THE SPINNING WHEELS MAKE IT DIFFICULT TO CHANGE DIRECTION, THE WHEELS BEHAVE JUST LIKE A TOY GYROSCOPE.

YOU MUST USE YOUR WEIGHT TO CHANGE DIRECTION.

SISSY SOON GOT THE HANG OF IT...

BRRRAAR

AFTER SISSY PASSED HER TEST WE WENT TO LOTS OF BIKE EVENTS.

BRAAAAR

WE SAW RACING BIKES THAT HAD TYRES WITH NO TREAD.

WHAT HAPPENS IF IT RAINS.

THEY HAVE TO USE TYRES WITH TREADS.

WE WENT TO A DRAG BIKE RACE. THIS IS WHERE SPECIALLY MADE BIKES RACE OVER A QUARTER MILE IN A STRAIGHT LINE.

WOW! THEY'RE VERY NOISY.

THAT'S BECAUSE THEY HAVE NO SILENCERS ON THE EXHAUST PIPES.

ROAAAR

WE SAW RIDERS PERFORM AMAZING STUNTS AT A SUPERCROSS FREESTYLE EVENT.

WOW! I BET THEY NEED GOOD SUSPENSION ON THOSE BIKES.

AT ONE EVENT WE SAW BIKES RACING ON ICE!

THE TYRES HAVE GOT SPIKES IN THEM TO GRIP THE ICE.

BUT OUR FAVOURITE EVENT WAS THE SHOW WHERE OWNERS SHOWED OFF THEIR OWN MOTORBIKES.

WOW! LOOK AT THAT CHOPPER.

WHY'S IT CALLED A CHOPPER?

BECAUSE IT'S MADE FROM CHOPPED UP PIECES.

THEY LIKED OUR BIKE BECAUSE IT WAS SO OLD. THEY CALLED IT A CLASSIC.

Parts of a motorbike

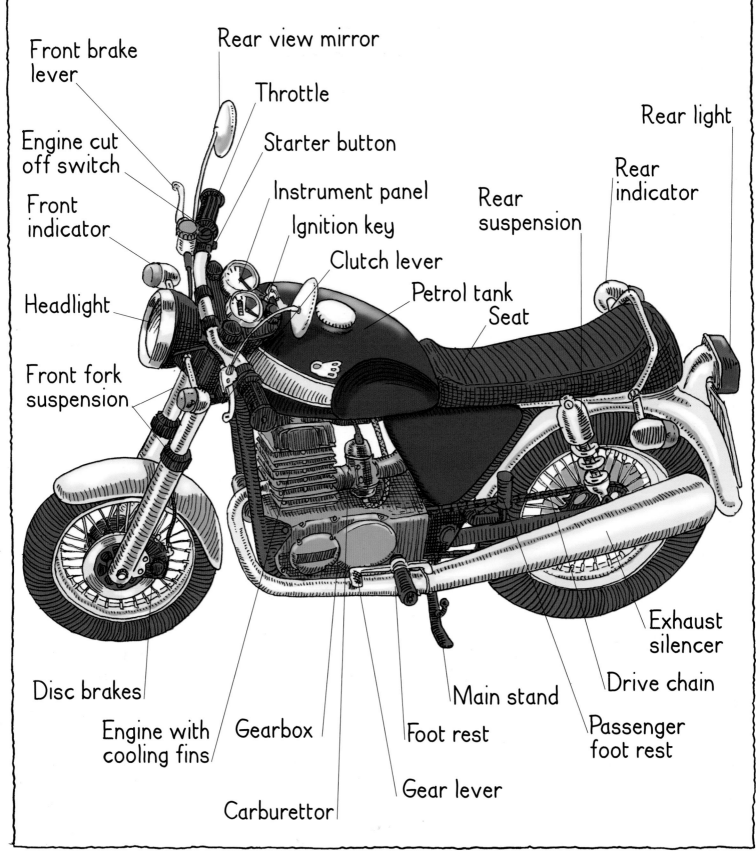

Front brake lever

Rear view mirror

Throttle

Starter button

Engine cut off switch

Front indicator

Instrument panel

Ignition key

Clutch lever

Rear suspension

Rear light

Rear indicator

Headlight

Petrol tank

Seat

Front fork suspension

Disc brakes

Engine with cooling fins

Gearbox

Carburettor

Gear lever

Foot rest

Main stand

Passenger foot rest

Drive chain

Exhaust silencer

Glossary

BATTERY
A DEVICE TO STORE ELECTRICITY. THE BATTERY PROVIDES POWER FOR THE STARTER MOTOR AND LIGHTS.

CABLE
A FLEXIBLE TUBE THAT CARRIES METAL WIRES OR BRAKE FLUID

CLUTCH
A METAL PLATE IN THE GEARBOX, WHICH RELEASES THE ENGINE'S POWER TO THE GEARS WHILE YOU CHANGE GEAR

CRANKSHAFT
THE ROTATING SHAFT AT THE BOTTOM OF THE ENGINE THAT IS TURNED BY THE PISTONS

DRIVE CHAIN
A SERIES OF LINKED PIECES OF METAL THAT FORMS A COMPLETE LOOP, WHICH CONNECTS THE DRIVE SPROCKET TO THE REAR WHEEL SPROCKET

ELECTRICITY
A FORM OF ENERGY THAT CAN MOVE AS A CURRENT ALONG A METAL WIRE TO POWER ELECTRICAL MACHINES

EXHAUST GASES
FUMES THAT ARE CREATED BY THE EXPLODING FUEL/AIR MIXTURE IN THE ENGINE

EXHAUST SILENCER
A DEVICE ON THE END OF THE EXHAUST PIPE, WHICH CUTS DOWN THE NOISE OF THE ESCAPING EXHAUST GASES

FRICTION
THE RESISTANCE BETWEEN TWO SURFACES RUBBING AGAINST EACH OTHER

FUEL
MATERIAL THAT IS BURNED FOR POWER. MOTORBIKE FUEL IS MADE FROM OIL.

GEARBOX
THE PLACE NEXT TO THE ENGINE WHERE THE GEARS ARE

IGNITE
TO SET ALIGHT

INTERNAL COMBUSTION ENGINE
AN ENGINE THAT PRODUCES POWER BY BURNING FUEL AND AIR INSIDE IT

LUBRICATE
TO MAKE SLIPPERY BY COVERING IN OIL OR GREASE

PISTON
A METAL CYLINDER THAT MOVES UP AND DOWN INSIDE ANOTHER CYLINDER

STALL
WHEN AN ENGINE STOPS BY ACCIDENT

STARTER MOTOR
AN ELECTRICAL DEVICE USED TO TURN THE CRANKSHAFT TO GET AN ENGINE STARTED

THROTTLE
THE DEVICE TO CONTROL THE AMOUNT OF FUEL INTO THE ENGINE. IT CONTROLS HOW FAST OR SLOW THE ENGINE SHOULD GO.

Index

A
AIR 10, 14
AXLE 18, 23

B
BATTERY 7, 11
BEARINGS 7, 18
BRAKE
    CALIPER 22, 23
    DISC 22, 23, 24
    PADS 22, 23
    REAR 26

C
CABLES 6
CARBURETTOR 6, 10, 30
CHOPPER 29
CLUTCH 15, 17, 26, 30
COMBUSTION CHAMBER 8
CRANKSHAFT 8, 10
CYLINDER 8, 9

D
DAMPER 24, 25
DRAG BIKE 28
DRIVE CHAIN 7, 16, 30

E
ELECTRICITY 12
ENGINE 8, 9, 10, 12, 13, 14,
    15, 16, 18, 30
ENGINE CUT OFF SWITCH
    30
EXHAUST 8, 9, 18, 19, 28,
    30
EXHAUST SILENCER 18, 19,
    28, 30

F
FINS 14, 30
FOOT REST 30
FORKS 24
FRICTION 18, 22, 23
FUEL 6, 9, 10, 11
    RESERVOIR 10
    TANK 6, 13, 30

G
GEARBOX 7, 14, 16
GEAR LEVER 30
GEARS 14, 15, 17
GREASE 16

H
HYDRAULIC FLUID 22, 23

I
IGNITION 30
INDICATOR
    FRONT 30
    REAR 30
    SWITCH 26
INLET 8
INSTRUMENT PANEL 30
INTERNAL COMBUSTION
    ENGINE 8

L
LIGHT
    HEADLIGHT 30
    REAR LIGHT 30

O
OIL 6, 13, 24, 25

P
PETROL 8, 10, 13, 30
PISTON 8, 9, 10, 22, 23
    CALIPER 22, 23

S
SEAT 30
SOOT 12
SPARK PLUGS 6, 9, 12
SPIKES 29
SPOKES 7, 19
SPROCKETS 16, 17
STALL 15
STAND 30
STARTER BUTTON 30
STARTER MOTOR 11
SUSPENSION 6, 24, 25,
    29
    FRONT 30
    REAR 30

T
THROTTLE 10, 11, 26, 30
TREAD 21
TWO-STROKE 8, 9, 13
TYRES 7, 20, 21, 28

W
WHEEL 7, 14, 16, 17, 18, 19,
    20, 23, 27
WHEEL HUB 18